IMAGES
of America

NILES
THE EARLY YEARS

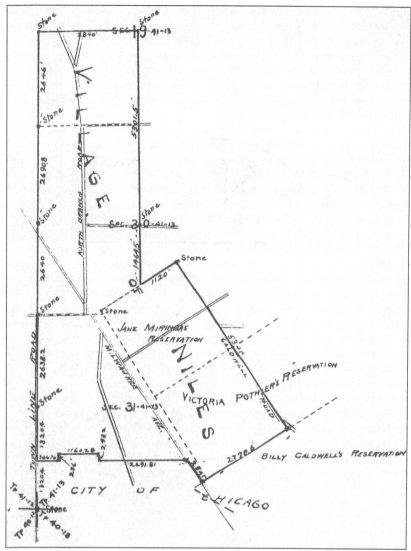

The original plat map of the village of Niles, Cook County, Illinois, was completed by surveyor C.N. Roberts on July 2, 1900, almost a year after the petition for incorporation was approved in Springfield on August 24, 1899. The newly incorporated village encompassed two large Potawatomi Indian reservations: the Jane Miranda and Victoria Pothier reserves. The land was purchased by the federal government on August 20, 1835, as a result of the Treaty of Prairie Du Chien in the territory of Michigan in 1829. (Courtesy of Niles Historical Society.)

ON THE COVER: The American Fireworks store at 6541 North Milwaukee Avenue, seen here about 1937, was the first of a string of roadside fireworks shops in the southern portion of the village, operating where Marcheschi Memorial Park currently marks the Chicago-Niles border. Chicagoans would flock to Niles to buy "loaded cigars," "auto bombs," and "repeating canes," because the sale of fireworks was illegal within the city limits. By 1939, thanks to a concentrated effort by the Illinois Society for the Prevention of Blindness, a statewide ban on the sale of fireworks was imminent. The population of Niles would remain at approximately 2,100 residents until after World War II. (Author's personal collection.)

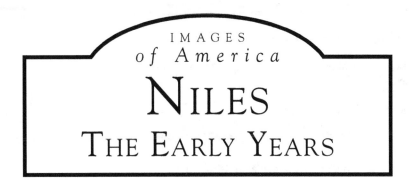

IMAGES
of America

NILES
THE EARLY YEARS

Thomas E. Ferraro

ARCADIA
PUBLISHING

Published by Arcadia Publishing
Charleston, South Carolina

Library of Congress Control Number: 2011945930

For all general information, please contact Arcadia Publishing:
Telephone 843-853-2070
Fax 843-853-0044
E-mail sales@arcadiapublishing.com
For customer service and orders:
Toll-Free 1-888-313-2665

Visit us on the Internet at www.arcadiapublishing.com

*This book is dedicated to
my friend and mentor,
Walter Beusse, a proud
member of "The Greatest
Generation," in recognition
of his more than 50 years of
tireless service to the Niles
community, and without
whom this book would
not have been possible.
Thank you, Walt.*

CONTENTS

ACKNOWLEDGMENTS

I owe an immeasurable debt of gratitude to Walter Beusse, president of the Niles Historical Society and Museum, for allowing me access to the photographic archives and historical collections housed at the museum, and for generously giving me his assistance and encouragement. Unless otherwise noted, the images appearing in this book were provided by the Niles Historical Society and Museum.

The late Ray Steil (1914–2011) was a one-of-a-kind Niles legend, and I am honored and privileged to have spent time in his company and reaped the benefits of his priceless memories and fascinating photos. Ray's son Robert "Bob" Steil is truly one of the nicest people I have ever met, and is a gentleman in every sense of the word. I hope this book is a fitting tribute to the memory of this remarkable man and the kindness of his son.

Andrew Schneider, former editor of the *Niles Bugle*, and current publisher and editor of *Screen* magazine, became my project manager when the chips were down and deserves no end of credit for his invaluable support and expertise.

Russ "Mr. Niles" McAndrew went above and beyond the call of duty by contributing original drawings of two notorious figures from Niles's distant past, in addition to one-of-a-kind material on Ilgair Park. I'm so glad to have met Russ! Local artist Gary Halverson stepped up to the plate when Russ's illness kept him from doing any further drawings. Gary saved the day by contributing three sketches of Prohibition-era policemen who played an important part in Niles history.

Many fine people have assisted me in various ways with this project, and I am grateful for their individual contributions. Specifically, I would like to thank Mayor Robert Callero, Ray Giovannelli, Ed Dennis, Bill Mehring, Lee Elsinger, Jim Kadlec, Ricky Chiero, Leonard and Dorothy Schiller, Clarence "Ben" Kath, Lois Wagner Kozeny, Debi Friedman, Russ Parker of the Elmwood Park Public Library, Patti Van Cleave of the Winnetka Historical Society, Thomas Smusyn, Tina Joern, Doris Gottschalk, Marty Stankowicz Sr., and Roman Szabelski, Phyllis Burns, and Diane Duerr of Catholic Cemeteries of Chicago.

My editor, Jeff Ruetsche, at Arcadia Publishing, deserves a medal for his endless supply of patience and support through several incarnations of this project. Thanks for making this happen, Jeff. I promised my daughter, Samantha, that I wouldn't forget that she scanned photos for me and endured the nighttime ghosts at the museum. I love you, Mini!

Finally, sometimes it seems like all of the good things in my life stem from the love and support of my incredible wife and partner, Julieann. Julie deserves to be co-author of this book, but is content to take payment in my undying devotion.

INTRODUCTION

Growing up in north-suburban Niles during the 1970s, I heard a lot of talk from the "old-timers" about the village's "shadowy" past. I had no idea what they were talking about, only that a place called "Joker Joe's" usually figured prominently in the cryptic fragments of information they were willing to provide. I imagined a wild past, filled with bootleggers, illegal gambling, and gangsters, having no idea how close to the truth I actually was.

I started my law enforcement career with the Niles Police Department in 1987 as a civilian desk officer. I was fortunate that when I got to the NPD, quite a few cops from the 1950s and 1960s were still on the force. I heard some great Niles stories, and my curiosity about my hometown and its history was piqued.

A few years ago, I read a book by a noted crime writer about Roger "The Terrible" Touhy, the bootlegger and racketeer who claimed Niles and the surrounding areas as his territory during Prohibition. This writer does not believe that Roger's brother Johnny was killed at the Lone Tree Tavern, then just outside of Niles, in 1927. I knew the writer was wrong, and I started doing some hardcore research to prove it. While spending hours online, going through an endless supply of archival newspaper articles from that era, I got more than I bargained for; there were dozens of articles about what was going on in Niles back then. I expanded my search to the years before and after the Volstead Act was being enforced, and turned up even more "lost" information. And thus, the idea for this book was born.

The village of Niles began as the pioneer settlement of Dutchman's Point on the north branch of the Chicago River during the Black Hawk War of 1832. The campfires of the recently exiled Potawatomi people were barely extinguished when John Schadiger and Julius Perren built their windowless log shanty near the remains of a native hunting camp on the east bank of the north branch of the Chicago River in present-day Niles. They may have been drawn to the abundant game and fertile soil found within the Miranda, Pothier, and Caldwell Indian reservations. A German pioneer named Nicholas Eckhoff settled on the river at the eastern juncture of the Pothier and Caldwell reservations, and took one or more Potawatomi wives. "Chief" Eckhoff's settlement may have been the first. It was referred to as Dutchman's Point by the sparse local population. Many more settlers, including the Ebinger, Plank, and Ruland families, would soon immigrate to the area around Dutchman's Point.

Niles Township was also born at Dutchman's Point, at the North Branch Hotel in 1850, and the little settlement gained some prominence as the town seat in the early years of the township's development. By 1880, Dutchman's Point was commonly being referred to as Niles, probably in reference to William Ogden Niles, the respected publisher of the *Niles Weekly Register*, a nationally acclaimed newspaper. In 1884, Niles boasted two stores, two hotels, one drug store, one harness shop, two blacksmith shops, three churches, two schools, one physician, and roughly 200 residents, predominantly of German and Scandinavian descent.

Incorporated in 1899, the new village's thriving business district was established along millionaire businessman Amos Snell's Northwest Plank Toll Road (later Milwaukee Avenue), in the area directly across from the recently consecrated St. Adalbert's Cemetery. Snell, one of the founders of Niles Township, would be murdered at his Chicago mansion in 1888; a sensational crime that was never solved. Every weekend, the picnic groves, saloons, and dance halls of Niles were packed with a mass exodus of Chicagoans, flocking to the adult amusements found just north of the city limits. By 1900, Chicago had extended the streetcar lines to a few blocks north of Devon Avenue, and this brought a major influx of Polish immigrants to Niles.

In 1911, an orphanage built to serve the needs of the Polish community of Chicago opened its doors at Park Ridge Road (Touhy Avenue) and Harlem Avenue in Niles. The Polish Manual Training School for Boys and St. Hedwig's Industrial School for Girls admitted its first charges on July 12, 1911. Taking up residence in the new brick building, the only structure of its size for miles, were 34 boys and 29 girls. Reverend Francis S. Rusch was the first superintendent and would remain in that position until his death in 1959. Father Rusch was assisted by the Felician Sisters, who taught school at the orphanage.

The residential staff of St. Hedwig's constituted a powerful voting bloc and had considerable impact on village elections. Father Rusch advocated the expansion of St. Adalbert's Cemetery and the acquisition of additional landholdings by the Archdiocese of Chicago. The village fathers were against this, instead hoping to develop more residential and business properties in the area of Milwaukee and Touhy Avenues. Ultimately, the Archdiocese was able to purchase over 250 acres of land adjacent to the cemetery and orphanage. According to John F. Calef (d. 1987), village president from 1923 to 1931, this was a primary reason why Niles has never had a recognizable "downtown" area.

During Prohibition, Niles was the gateway to "Rural Bohemia," the roadhouse district of suburban speakeasies and resorts during the beer wars between gangsters Roger Touhy and Al Capone. Although Niles did not have the largest number of roadhouses within its corporate limits—that distinction belonged to neighboring Morton Grove—it certainly had its share of murder, mayhem, and scandals. In spite of this fact, the village was slowly but surely making the climb to respectability, a journey that would take several decades of hard work and perseverance by a core group of honest and hardworking people.

George S. May's Tam O'Shanter Country Club, which some call the birthplace of modern professional golf, rose to international prominence in Niles during the Great Depression and continued to host the sport's most exclusive and highest-paying contests until well after World War II. May was known as the "P.T. Barnum of Golf" for his high-rolling ways and elaborate publicity stunts, including offering unheard-of cash prizes to the winners.

Behind the village's colorful and sometimes checkered past, another Niles existed, grounded by strong agrarian values and a deep sense of community pride: the truck farms of Maine and Niles Townships. These gentleman farmers and their families formed the backbone of local society and culture, and their influence on Niles is still felt today. They were especially important considering that almost everything north of Oakton Street was once farmland.

In 2010, the village of Niles was voted "Best Place to Raise Your Kids" by *Bloomberg Businessweek* magazine, for towns with populations under 50,000. The magazine gives Niles the top honor in Illinois, but also suggests that Niles may be the best place in the country to raise children. This well-deserved distinction makes me very proud.

My intention with this book has been to tell what happened in Niles in the past so that we can understand how Niles came to be what it is today. A second book covering 1955–present is already in the works; please contact me at NilesPhotoBook@yahoo.com for further information.

One

DUTCHMAN'S POINT

This photograph looking north at the intersection of the Northwest Plank Road (Milwaukee Avenue) and North Branch Road (Waukegan Road), was taken during the summer of 1911 or earlier. Young August Kadlec stands by a deep well; the White House Tavern, in continuous operation as a public house from the 1830s until it was demolished in 1964, is in the background at right. The tavern in Dutchman's Point was a resting place for Native Americans carrying their canoes from the North Branch of the Chicago River to the Des Plaines River. The pole and building at the far left is roughly where Paul Rybski's Marathon service station stands today.

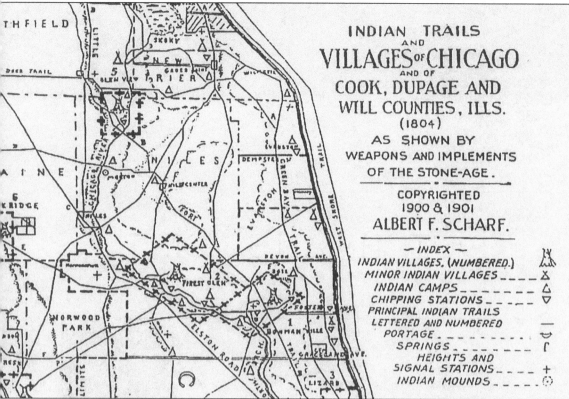

Albert Frederick Scharf (1847–1929) was a local historian who made a lifetime study of the Native American presence in northern Illinois. This segment of his map, and the corresponding entry in the Scharf manuscript, indicate that "Between the Elston Road Trail C, and the river, in Sec 32, town Niles, there was a minor Indian village as an out-post of the main village on the west" and that this "minor Indian village is known to our pioneers as 'Dutchman's Point' referring to a German by the name of Eckhof who was one of the latter day Potawatomi Chiefs with Indian wives." This information states definitively that Dutchman's Point was named for Eckhof. An 1851 map of Niles Township includes the name "Eckhof" at the eastern juncture of the Pothier and Caldwell reservations. Scharf unknowingly named Eckhof the de facto founder of Niles. The township's tax records for 1854 include a Nicholas Eckhoff, who was said to have lived on the north branch of the Chicago River. (Courtesy of the Winnetka Historical Society.)

RiverScene Niles.Ill.

This historical postcard from around 1900 shows the approximate site on the north branch of the Chicago River where John Schadiger and Julius Perren built the first log cabin in 1832, within the boundaries of what is now Niles. Schadiger soon left the area for Wisconsin, but Perren stayed in Niles until his death in 1873. At right are Barbara and Christian Ebinger, who in 1834, along with John Plank, settled and farmed the land now largely occupied by St. Adalbert's Cemetery. The Ebingers and Planks were known for their hospitality, and were always willing to provide food and lodging to weary overnight travelers. Christian Ebinger was elected township assessor and overseer of the poor in 1850.

The Kadlec family arrived from the historical kingdom of Bohemia—now the Czech Republic—in the 19th century, eventually settling in Niles on this farm in the 7200 block of North Milwaukee Avenue. Kadlecs still operate a business at 7254 North Milwaukee Avenue; they are one of the only original Niles families to remain in continuous possession of the same land. The house pictured below was at one time believed to be the oldest frame structure in the village. It was originally owned by a Mr. Brunst, followed by August Kadlec Jr., and finally Thomas Kadlec Sr., who owned it until it was torn down in the latter part of the 20th century. The house had previously been a dance hall and store.

The two-story building on the left is Fred Mau's shoe store, on the northwest corner of Milwaukee Avenue and Park Ridge Road (Touhy Avenue). The building later became the State Bank of Niles. August C. Kadlec Sr.'s Niles Home Bakery sits next door, although it would later be rebuilt on the south side of the bank. The Niles Hotel on North Branch Road (Waukegan Road) is visible in the background, behind the bakery. The two-story, square building behind the sign for the Niles Hotel (below) is believed to be the original North Branch Hotel, birthplace of Niles Township. The North Branch Hotel was built and operated by John Marshall and Benjamin Hall in 1837. By 1884, it was owned by Amos Snell and operated by Daniel Stryker. The pre-1905 view looks east; the white house in the far background is on Park Ridge Road, approximately where the entrance to the Renaissance Condominiums on Touhy Avenue is today.

August Kadlec's Niles Home Bakery delivery wagon takes out an order around 1910. The Kadlec family delivered bread and baked goods from the southern end of the village. Farther north, near Oakton Street, dairy farmer Theodore Pollex delivered milk and cream from his horse-drawn wagon. Below is the stately, red-brick home of Frank and Nellie Whittington as it appeared in 1880. (Note the hitching post for horse and buggy.) The Whittingtons were a prominent Dutchman's Point family, active in both the social and political scenes of Niles Township. Their estate was located near the present-day intersection of Howard Street and Waukegan Road.

Englishman Benjamin Lupton (1817–1894) arrived in Dutchman's Point in 1840 with his wife, Mary Arrowsmith Lupton. Lupton worked as the settlement's blacksmith for the next 20 years, operating on the large tract of land he owned between North Branch Road and the Northwest Plank Road. Dr. Theodore Hoffman (below) was born in 1820 in Hamburg, Germany and educated at Heidelberg before coming to America to finish his studies at Rush Medical College. Dr. Hoffman came to Dutchman's Point in 1849 and practiced medicine throughout northern Cook and southern Lake Counties until 1868, when he moved to Chicago. In 1871, the Great Chicago Fire destroyed his office and four houses, so he moved back to his home on North Branch Road, near the present-day St. Michael's Orthodox Catholic Church, where he continued to practice medicine until his death in 1905.

Frank Whittington arrived in Dutchman's Point in 1870 and was a friend and neighbor of Benjamin Lupton, later serving as Niles's first commissioner of streets. He owned a stately farm near the intersection of what is now Waukegan Road and Howard Street. In 1893, *The Chicago Tribune* reported that Whittington and other trustees of the Niles Township Board of Drainage were being sued to prove by what authority they levied special tax assessments for farm drainage. Whittington's wife, Nellie (left), was a prominent member of society in Niles, performing in local theater productions, organizing scrap metal drives for the Red Cross during World War I, and serving on the Niles District 71 School Board well into the 1920s.

In 1858, the *Tribune* reported that there was a "grand rally at Dutchman's Point, and the voters of Niles are, almost to a man, in favor of Lincoln." John H. Calef of Maine Township (right) enlisted in the 88th Illinois Infantry in 1861, at the start of the Civil War. He was seriously wounded in the Battle of Missionary Ridge, and by 1865, had received a battlefield commission for bravery. He returned home, only to die in the smallpox epidemic of 1871. His son, John L. Calef, born six days after his father's death, is shown below around 1907 with his wife, Caroline, and their children, John F. and Katherine L. "Kit" Calef. John L. became arguably Dutchman's Point's most prominent businessman in the late 1800s. He was an early Niles postmaster, as well as one of the founders of Niles Volunteer Fire Company.

John L. Calef and his family posed in front of their Home Buffet Restaurant and Tavern at 7105 North Milwaukee Avenue around 1903. The small white addition to the right of the main building served as both the ladies entrance to the bar and the post office. Calef had Niles's first telephone installed at this location—the extension was "Niles No. 1." Below, John L. Calef and James Haag tend bar to a group including Mark Haag, the Maine Township marshal, identifiable by his uniform coat and star, and Henry Bierschwale, the first police magistrate of Niles and the owner of a hardware store at 7146 North Milwaukee Avenue, seated at left.

In 1870, John S. Niemann came to Dutchman's Point from Alborg, Denmark, and within a year, purchased a thriving saloon and dance hall at 7139 North Milwaukee Avenue from his employer, Peter Thorsen. "Niemann's Place" later expanded, with a picnic grove behind the popular establishment. Niemann eventually became a village trustee and treasurer of the volunteer fire company. He is shown here beside his 1916 Denby truck. Below, a group of men pose in front of Niemann's Place around 1910. Note the pistol being brandished by the man on the far left. In 1908, eight-year-old John Dowe was killed by a stray revolver bullet fired by an unknown person in Niles. Sad events such as this accentuated the need for an organized police force in the coming years.

August C. Kadlec Jr., the Niles Township constable, walks the snowy pathways of St. Adalbert's Cemetery prior to World War I. A line of taverns on Milwaukee Avenue is visible just outside the cemetery fence to the right. Prior to the 1920s, law enforcement in Dutchman's Point and Niles was a fragmented affair, consisting of township constables and marshals, special policemen, volunteer policemen, and the Cook County sheriff.

Looking north from 7105 North Milwaukee Avenue in 1903, Niles featured, from the right foreground to the far distance, John L. Calef's Home Buffet, an adjoining horse shelter, the front yard of the Calef home at 7107 North Milwaukee Avenue, possibly John L. Calef's Niles Center Mercantile Company, Charlie Schickinger's bicycle shop, Niemann's Place, an unknown building, and, in the far background at right, Nick Roh's grocery store. Note the wagon ruts in the dirt road.

St. John's Lutheran Church, located at 7429 North Milwaukee Avenue, was formally organized on January 12, 1859. The parsonage, seen here with the church in 1902, was built in 1894 on land donated by brewer William Lill, and still stands. The historic church was destroyed by fire in its centennial year, 1959, and subsequently rebuilt. German services were offered until 1950, when all services became English-speaking only.

Students of St. John's Lutheran School pose with their headmaster in 1896. In 1872, the first school building, a two-story frame affair, was built on land donated by the congregation. Classes were held on the first floor and the teacher's quarters were located upstairs. Also known as the "German School," enrollment was 115 pupils in 1874, including 83 members of the congregation.

Benjamin Lupton was "saved" at a revival meeting of the Methodist Evangelical Church at Dutchman's Point in 1870. He donated the land on which this church stands, at 7339 North Waukegan Road, stipulating that a trust be established mandating that the parcel remain sacred ground. The congregation remained active until 1920, when a saloonkeeper attempted to buy the property. Matilda Schwinge successfully sued to have the building remain a church. Today, it is the First Baptist Church of Niles.

The first one-room schoolhouse in Dutchman's Point was located near today's intersection of Touhy and Harlem Avenues in 1838. There were four students—two each from the Ebinger and Ruland families. In 1849, John Odell donated land for a new school near Milwaukee and Harlem Avenues. In 1894, the school was relocated to the present location of Niles Elementary School-South at 6935 West Touhy Avenue, and by 1916, this building had been erected on what was then School Street.

Two

THE NEW VILLAGE

On August 24, 1899, Dutchman's Point, known casually as Niles since before the Civil War, officially incorporated as the Village of Niles. John Huntington, Niles Township supervisor in 1875 and 1876, was chosen to be the first village president. He operated a horse-drawn omnibus that carried passengers from Niles to downtown Chicago for a round-trip fare of 70¢. The first village board consisted of trustees Charles Anderson, Henry Thoms, Thomas Day, William G. Brown, August Habedank, and C.T. Tarnow. Fred Mau was appointed village clerk, Christ Thorsen was appointed treasurer, and Frank Whittington was appointed commissioner of streets. Joseph F. Stoelting's blacksmith shop, located on the east side of Milwaukee Avenue between Kozla's cigar factory and Nick Roh's grocery store, is shown above c. 1910. Stoelting was elected police magistrate in 1906.

In 1896, a group poses in front of John L. Calef's store. They are, from left to right, John Huntington; John L. Calef; William Brown, a future trustee; John Ruland, a descendent of Revolutionary War heroes and son of John Jackson Ruland and Hannah Ketchum Ruland, prominent early settlers of Dutchman's Point; and Ernest Moss, who worked at the Union Stock Yards in Chicago and lived at the White House Tavern on Milwaukee Avenue. John Huntington retired to Kenosha, Wisconsin, in 1903 and lived to age 96.

John L. Calef, with hands on hips, stands in front of his first tavern, a two-story, brick building built before 1900 at 7052 North Milwaukee Avenue, on the west side of the street. Calef later sold this building to Elmer Kessel, who opened a grocery store on the premises. Elmer's brother, Irving Kessel, owned a tavern on the southeast corner of Milwaukee and Touhy Avenues. The building at 7052 North Milwaukee Avenue would eventually gain notoriety as Joker Joe's Typhoon Club. Habedank's Butcher Shop and Meat Market, owned by inaugural trustee Gus Habedank, was located just north of this building.

On April 22, 1915, a thousand people gathered in Niles to celebrate the concrete paving of four miles of Milwaukee Avenue from the end of the streetcar line in Chicago north through the village limits and beyond to Northfield Township. The cost was $14,000 per mile. Above, Miss Jeanette Pohlman christens the pavement with a bottle of champagne. Below, Cook County board president Peter Reinberg symbolically removes the last shovelful of dirt from the construction project. The refinishing of Milwaukee Avenue would bring Niles closer to recognition as a settled community, rather than as an uncivilized mecca of bars and taverns surrounded by farmland.

Niles policeman John Wagner was photographed in 1901 when his title was "Special Policeman," an unpaid position created to assist the village marshal, who was paid on a per-arrest basis. Self-serving saloonkeepers routinely appointed special policemen to satisfy the village ordinance requiring a police presence at every event for which a permit was issued and at which alcohol was served, but Wagner was a genuine volunteer lawman who wore Star No. 1 in addition to being the resident engineer at St. Adalbert's cemetery.

The Niles Volunteer Fire Company was formally organized in 1901 under Frank Lenzen, the first fire marshal. The company was officially recognized in a charter granted by Illinois Secretary of State James A. Rose on February 19, 1912. This photograph, from July 4, 1915, shows members, from left to right, Tony Tenhopen, John F. Calef, Ed Thomas, Lou Kozla, and driver Bill Habedank.

August and Rozalia Kadlec's bakery, seen here around 1915, was later expanded by their son, Tom Kadlec, to include an ice cream parlor and renamed Rosie's Sweet Shoppe after his mother. Fred Mau's shoe store, which would become the State Bank of Niles in 1921, is in the background.

In 1902, Fire Marshal Frank Lenzen's blacksmith shop was on the west side of Milwaukee Avenue at Harts Road. In later years, his son, John (far left) would transition from wagons and buggies to automobiles, running a garage at this location. His other son, Frank Jr. (next to John) owned and operated Lenzen's Town Tavern across the street at 7015 North Milwaukee Avenue, the future location of "Go To Blase's."

Trustee Charles Anderson, seen here in his Masonic Knights Templar uniform, became Niles's third president in 1902. When he came to town as a retired businessman in 1899, the population was 200, and when he left office in 1907, there were well over 500 residents. By 1912, Anderson was living on his farm at the northwest corner of Oakton Street and North Branch (Waukegan) Road.

John F. Calef (1897–1987), son of John L. Calef, was photographed after enlisting during World War I. He graduated from Niles Elementary School before attending Carl Schurz High School in Chicago. He would eventually earn a bachelor's degree in chemistry, after attending both Northwestern University and the University of Chicago. Calef worked in his father's restaurant as a boy, and also weeded onion fields for local farmers. In 1923, he became Niles's fifth president.

Fred Beisswanger came to Niles Township from Germany in 1883 and engaged in a notoriously corrupt "speed trap" extortion racket from 1906 to 1911, preying on unsuspecting motorists to pad his pockets with "out-of-court" settlements, or bribes. He got himself "elected" a Cook County justice of the peace and established his "courtroom" on the second floor of Kuchna's Tavern, illegally appointing constables to assist him in his scam. Beisswanger's antics earned him a grand jury indictment for malfeasance; he barely managed to avoid prosecution, resigning from office in the courtroom of Cook County Judge John E. Owens, who dismissed the case under the stipulation that Beisswanger would make restitution, which he never did. Beisswanger managed to keep the scam going, using local Niles businessman Frank Karlovsky as his "patsy" justice of the peace, and acting as Karlovsky's "clerk." Beisswanger was facing prison time for extorting immigrants on trumped-up Prohibition charges and impersonating a federal judge when he was struck and killed by a speeding hit-and-run driver in 1923. (Original drawing by Russ McAndrew from the author's personal collection.)

This photograph from before World War I shows what is believed to be Kuchna's Tavern at 6839 North Milwaukee Avenue, one of the earliest public houses in incorporated Niles, dating from the late 1800s. The building was later the Silver Leaf and the House of Tromba before becoming Przybylo's House of the White Eagle. A portion of the structure was incorporated into the modernization of the White Eagle and still stands today.

Frank Karlovsky (standing, second from left), a stonecutter by trade, worked at the Anton Sochurek Monument Works in the 6700 block of Evergreen Street. He married his boss's daughter, Mary (standing, far left), who ran her family's tavern and restaurant at 6705 North Evergreen Street (behind them). In 1913, Karlovsky became embroiled in the "Niles Auto Mill" bribery scandal perpetuated by Fred Beisswanger after becoming a justice of the peace and allowing Beisswanger to serve as his clerk. The two operated their kangaroo court out of the Sochurek's tombstone shop. Arraigned for extortion, Karlovsky admitted to the court that he knew "nothing about the law." He died soon after, on October 17, 1915.

The town gathers for a Fourth of July parade at the intersection of Milwaukee Avenue, Park Ridge Road (now Touhy Avenue), and Evergreen Street in 1918. Above, looking south, the pavilion in the foreground stands approximately where the Veteran's Memorial waterfall is located today. The small white building to the right was the first village hall and jail and the adjacent brown-brick building was Bierschwale's Hardware Store, which would later become the Burgundy Inn. The white shed under the bell tower housed "Blue Boy," the fire department's first hand-operated pumper. The man on the right, near the flag, is standing on the roof of the Kadlec Bakery. The scene on the ground is shown below with Niles's second and fourth village president, Fred Mau, addressing the crowd from the makeshift stage. In 1915, Mau ordered Niles's nine saloons closed on Sundays, an unpopular decision in a town described by the *Tribune* as the "wettest place on the map."

Sailors from the Great Lakes naval base dress their lines in front of the Mike Usis Dry Goods Store at 7205 North Milwaukee Avenue in preparation for the Fourth of July parade in 1918. The veiled ladies in the background are Red Cross volunteers. John F. Calef and his wife lived in an apartment above this store when they were newlyweds. In 1924, A.P. Gronau opened the Niles Pharmacy at this location, selling it to Mark Toepel in 1930, who renamed it M. Toepel's Drugs.

A truck carrying a replica Liberty Bell travels northbound in front of Irving E. Kessel's saloon during the parade. In 1918, this reproduction bell and others like it were featured in parades to promote the US Treasury's War Savings Stamps program, a patriotic effort aimed at schoolchildren to help fund participation in World War I. Kozla's cigar factory, Stoelting's blacksmith shop, and Roh's grocery are visible just south of Kessel's on Milwaukee Avenue. Kessel's Saloon would become an Arco gas station at the corner of Milwaukee and Touhy Avenues in the 1970s.

Three

St. Adalbert's Cemetery

St. Adalbert (956–997), the Czech Roman Catholic bishop of Prague, was martyred during his missionary efforts to convert the Baltic Prussians. He is the patron saint of Bohemia, Hungary, Poland, and Prussia. In 1872, two prominent Catholic priests, Father Adolph Bakanowski (Congregation of the Resurrection), pastor of the Polish St. Stanislaus Kostka Church, and Father Joseph Molitor, pastor of the Czech St. Wenceslaus Bohemian Church, joined together to facilitate a loan of between $5,500 and $10,000 from Chapek and Associates of Chicago for the purchase of anywhere from 16 to 21 acres of land along Milwaukee Avenue for an Ethnic-Slavic Catholic cemetery. First known as "Bohemian Polish Cemetery," St. Adalbert's didn't keep on-site records until 1912, when the office pictured here was erected on Milwaukee Avenue. Note Xavery Wojkiewicz's greenhouses to the left. Wojkiewicz emigrated from Poland in 1888 and became the official grave decorator at St. Adalbert's.

This historical postcard from around 1914 shows the original entrance to the cemetery, south of the current main gate. At that time, the cemetery only extended north as far as the current location of the White Eagle Restaurant. The first executive director, Monsignor Thomas Bona, was appointed in 1912 and served continuously until his death in 1950. Edmund Zwiardowski was the superintendent in 1892. Paul M. Williams was serving in that post in 1916. Julius Szatkowski was appointed superintendent in 1921, and served until 1951. Szatkowski is credited with expanding the cemetery to its current geographic boundaries. Additionally, roads were paved, curbs were installed, damaged benches and rusted iron fences were replaced or removed, the landscaping was extensively overhauled, and storm sewers were installed to prevent flooding.

A horse-drawn funeral carriage stops on a curving path in the cemetery around 1900. In the early days of the cemetery, Milwaukee Avenue was paved only as far as Lawrence Avenue and it became a muddy, rutted quagmire as it progressed north into Niles. It was not uncommon for a hearse being pulled by a team of spirited horses to get stuck in the deep wagon tracks and overturn.

A hearse prepares to enter the cemetery in 1914, the same year the brick office to the left of the entrance was built. Pavel's Ice Cream Parlor, in the foreground to the immediate right, was originally built to house the first cemetery office in 1912. The greenhouse south of Pavel's belonged to Xavier Wojkiewicz, a Polish immigrant who settled in Niles in 1896 and gained prominence as the cemetery's official grave decorator and a village trustee.

Once a thriving industry in Niles, by 1946 only Patek and Sons at 6723 North Milwaukee Avenue, Joseph Vosmik & Sons at 6875 North Milwaukee Avenue and Kuper Monumental Works (shown) at 6605 North Milwaukee Avenue were still making tombstones locally. Today, only Patek and Sons remains, and it is one of the oldest continuously operating businesses in Niles.

Frank X. Stankowicz, father of Niles's eighth village president, Frank J. Stankowicz, stands second from the left in the first row at St. Adalbert's Cemetery around 1900. In 1901, Frank X. Stankowicz was also a policeman without pay. Frances Molitor and her father are standing to the immediate right of Stankowicz. Mr. Molitor appears to have been the head grave digger, and was probably related to Rev. Joseph Molitor, one of the founders of the cemetery. In 1943, striking grave diggers blocked 15 funerals at the main gate; they were seeking a raise from 75¢ to 95¢ an hour.

Engineers hired by St. Adalbert's Cemetery were allowed to live in this water tower located in the 6700 block of Newark Avenue, on the west side of the cemetery. Water was supplied to the cemetery by a 1,300-foot-deep, steam-powered well. Engineer John Wagner, also a volunteer policeman, lived in the tower with his family in the early 20th century.

Joseph Vosmik (above, standing second from left) leans on a piece of stonework in front of his stonecutting and monument works in the 6800 block of North Milwaukee Avenue in 1905. Vosmik's shop is shown below around 1940.

Located just north of the current administration building at St. Adalbert's Cemetery, this bronze and granite World War I monument is a Niles landmark. Commissioned by the Polish-American Gold Star Father's and Mother's Association, the monument was dedicated on July 4, 1928, in a ceremony attended by His Eminence, George Cardinal Mundelein. There are four statues, honoring the Army, the Navy, the Marine Corps, and the Polish Army in France, also known as "Haller's Army," after commanding general Jozef Haller. (Courtesy of Catholic Cemeteries.)

The Spanish Influenza epidemic of 1918 resulted in 4,000 burials at St. Adalbert's. In 1923, under the leadership of newly appointed superintendent Julius Szatkowski, the cemetery underwent a major renovation and beautification program, which ultimately led to the construction of this distinctive, Spanish Mission–style administration building. (Courtesy of Catholic Cemeteries.)

Four

St. Hedwig's
Industrial School

In 1906, Archbishop James E. Quigley of Chicago saw the need for a new Catholic orphanage to care for the sizable number of Polish orphans in public institutions around the city. The Polish-American parishes responded with generous financial contributions, and in 1910, Polish auxiliary bishop Paul Rhode oversaw the construction of a four-story building on 17 acres at what is now Touhy and Harlem Avenues, near St. Adalbert's Cemetery. The original building, 7135 North Harlem Avenue, was divided into two sections, "The Polish Manual Training School for Boys" and "St. Hedwig's Industrial School for Girls." In 1911, the cornerstone was laid and Father (later Monsignor) Francis S. Rusch (1884–1959) was appointed superintendent. The Felician Sisters provided 15 nuns to live and teach at the new orphanage. On July 12, 1911, 63 Polish orphans—34 boys and 29 girls—were transferred from St. Joseph's Home in Avondale to St. Hedwig's. St. Hedwig of Silesia (1174–1243), the institution's namesake, was a Polish Duchess canonized in 1267. The original construction crew, largely comprised of stonecutters and masons from local Niles shops, is shown here around 1911.

Monsignor Rusch, shown here with the class of 1941, was a cigar-chomping disciplinarian with a kind heart and a taste for fairness and Fox Deluxe beer. He rarely went anywhere without "Duke," his huge Dalmatian, an ill-tempered beast with crude habits. Reverend Rusch was well-known—and well-loved—by his charges for being able to say the Tridentine Latin Mass in just under 22 minutes. Rusch gave 48 years of his life as superintendent of St. Hedwig's. He despised the word "orphanage," preferring to view his domain as a boarding school and loving home to the children under his care. St. Hedwig's became a fully developed, 41-acre campus under Rusch's leadership, as seen in the historical postcard below from around 1930.

Sister Mary Dulcis is reading nursery rhymes to preschool and kindergarten students on June 1, 1949; the young kids had mentors from the upper classes assigned to their dormitories to assist the nuns with their care. One of the perks of this duty was that the teenaged assistants were allowed to eat with the younger students; it was well known that the young kids' food was much more appetizing than the meals served to their older counterparts. The downside was that the mentor was required to sleep in the youngsters' dormitory and comfort them in the event of a nightmare. Starting in 1930, adventurous older students would sneak off campus to Toepel's Drug Store at Milwaukee and Touhy Avenues for sodas, candy, and other swag. Construction of the gymnasium (shown below in a historic postcard) was begun in 1930 and completed in 1933. The modern brick structure was the only one of its kind for miles—Niles did not have (and has never had) a public high school. (Both, author's personal collection)

Strict segregation of the sexes was enforced at St. Hedwig's, with one notable exception: the popular marching band, shown here around 1940. On November 11, 1918, at 5:30 a.m., members of the marching band, learning that World War I had ended, broke into the music room and took possession of their instruments and an American flag. They then paraded down Milwaukee Avenue, shouting, "The war is over!" to the sleepy residents. Following World War I, the orphanage took on an additional 130 girls, all of them Siberian war refugees.

Every second and fourth Sunday of the month was designated a "Visiting Sunday" for relatives of the residents. The children would report to their respective dayrooms in their Sunday best, and receive their visitors between 1:00 p.m. and 5:00 p.m. All outdoor activities were prohibited on visiting days. Sadly, many orphans never received a visitor at St. Hedwig's, and these Sundays were especially cruel for them.

Sisters Mary De Pazzi (left) and Mary Leonette chaperoned a group of boys and girls from St. Hedwig's to the Hawthorn-Mellody Farms dairy and petting zoo in Libertyville, Illinois, on August 13, 1948. It was the first time many of the children had seen a goat in person.

Robert G. Friedman was a distinguished member of the class of 1947 and is seen here as a young lieutenant in the US Army Signal Corps. Friedman would rise to the rank of lieutenant colonel and see action in both Korea and Vietnam before retiring from the service.

Sports were very popular at St. Hedwig's, especially baseball, at both the intramural and varsity levels. It was not uncommon for tightly contested intramural games to last for hours, with the priests and staff playing on teams with the students. The campus was home to a regulation baseball diamond, the finest field in the surrounding area. In the late 1930s and early 1940s, St. Hedwig's baseball teams engaged in interleague play with other schools, and played exhibition games against traveling club and barnstorming teams, including the Niles Tigers. Here, Frank Grzempa, class of 1942, poses in his brown and cream "Apaches" uniform, possibly representing Holy Trinity High School in Chicago. (Boys from St. Hedwig's attended their junior and senior years of high school at Holy Trinity, while the girls went to Good Counsel High School, also in Chicago.)

Excited students from St. Hedwig's Industrial School raced to board a helicopter at Meigs Field for a ride to Midway Airport on September 28, 1958. They were guests of the Chicago Junior Association of Commerce and Industry. These young flyers had an unexpected thrill when they witnessed a DC-7 passenger plane limp into Midway with a dead engine.

Every year at Christmastime, the local American Legion sponsored a much-anticipated holiday program at St. Hedwig's. Members served the children a special Christmas meal and passed out presents and candy after dinner. There was also entertainment, usually a Christmas pageant or concert, and the boys and girls would sing Christmas carols. In this festive scene from around 1950, a legionnaire looks on while one of the priests plays Santa Claus.

Monsignor Rusch keeps order while Bob Ord, the local Goebel beer distributor, passes out the soda pop he donated for the summer picnic on the grounds of St. Hedwig's on July 13, 1952. Another popular summer activity at the orphanage was the annual trip to Camp Villa Marie, a summer camp run by Catholic charities on the Pistakee Bay in Johnsburg, Illinois.

Actress Betty Hutton joins a group of happy youngsters from St. Hedwig's at a performance of the Cole Brothers Circus on April 30, 1953. Generous charitable donations from groups and individuals made off-campus field trips like this one possible. Below, Sister Dulcis watches as her kindergartners play with Tinker Toys on May 10, 1948. (Both, author's personal collection.)

William B. Schmidt, owner of the Riverview Amusement Park at Western and Belmont Avenues in Chicago, watches as an excited group of kids from St. Hedwig's and their Felician chaperones storm the park on opening day, May 14, 1960; this was the final time the Hedwigians enjoyed this annual free outing, as the orphanage closed later that year due to a lack of need because of increased adoptions and diminished enrollment.

This view looks north across the front of St. Hedwig's Industrial School sometime after World War II, with Alberding's Mobil Station at 7201 North Harlem Avenue barely visible in the background. St. Hedwig's only offered schooling through 10th grade, so the boys completed their junior and senior years at Holy Trinity High School in Chicago and the girls at Good Counsel High School, also on the north side of Chicago. On January 11, 1953, a fire broke out in the closet of a sewing room at St. Hedwig's (below). The Niles Fire Department was assisted by firefighters from Chicago and eight municipalities. No one was injured in the fire, which caused $40,000 in damage to the aging structure. *The Tribune* reported that at the time of the fire, the school housed 183 boys and 140 girls, ranging in age from 2 to 16. The venerable Niles institution closed less than eight years later. (Courtesy of Park Ridge Historical Society.)

Five

PROHIBITION AND
THE DEPRESSION ERA

On the morning of November 11, 1921, 200 Gold Star Mothers gathered at the intersection of Milwaukee Avenue and Waukegan Road to dedicate a monument in memory of their sons. A heavy bronze plaque affixed to a granite base displayed the names of 240 American servicemen from the northern Chicago area who lost their lives in World War I. Following a somber ceremony conducted by the American Legion, Boy Scouts from Troops 869 and 870 worked until after nightfall to plant 240 "Memory Trees"—an elm, black walnut, or maple for each man on the plaque—moving north on Waukegan Road from the starting point in Niles, and not stopping until the last tree was planted. The historic monument, shown here around 1925, has been lost to history and its fate and whereabouts are unknown. Additionally, not a single Memory Tree remains marked or designated along Waukegan Road.

Frank and Mary Tomaszewski stand in front of their Marvel Inn Tavern and Picnic Grove at 6873 North Milwaukee Avenue around 1930. This building was originally an ice cream parlor owned by Mary's parents, Joe and Emma Vosmik, and is one of the few early-20th-century brick structures remaining in Niles. Immediately to the north was a grocery store once owned by Judge Joseph Jozwiak, and now known as The Chambers Restaurant at 6881 North Milwaukee Avenue. The Florentine Restaurant (below), seen here around 1930, was formerly John L. Calef's Home Buffet & Tavern. Although John L. Calef was listed in the census of 1920, he died shortly thereafter. His son, John F. Calef, would become the acting village president in 1923, replacing the retiring Fred Mau.

The Cook County Highway Police were formally organized in 1923 during the scandal-ridden administration of Sheriff Peter M. Hoffman. Shortly after their inception, this police station, seen here around 1950, was built for them at 8970 North Milwaukee Avenue, in what was then considered East Maine, with a Morton Grove mailing address. The Babcock Garage (later C. Swenson Paints) at 8980 North Milwaukee Avenue is the white building to the north of the sign. During Prohibition, almost everything north of Howard Street fell under Cook County's police jurisdiction. Below, Sergeant Jimmy Allegretti of the Cook County Highway Police poses in front of the sheriff's station in August 1941. The view looks east toward Washington Street before Ballard Road extended east across Milwaukee Avenue. Allegretti would serve with distinction from 1928 until World War II, when he entered the Army. His brother, Dr. Leonard Allegretti, maintained a dental office in Lawrencewood for many years.

Peter Oszakowski became the Niles chief of police in 1924, succeeding Canadian-born Clarence Van Dusen, who had held that position since 1916. His sporadic tenure through the 1920s was plagued with scandal, and even made national news. Oszakowski's brother, Mike, owned the Avenue Tavern on Milwaukee Avenue and was the political boss of Niles, overseeing bootlegging operations in the area. Pete is shown here in front of Kozla's Barber Shop at Milwaukee and Touhy Avenues in 1924. He was convicted of attempting to bribe Prohibition agents under Elliot Ness's predecessor in Chicago and sentenced to prison at Leavenworth, Kansas.

Fred Mau, both the second and fourth village president, converted his shoe store into the first National Bank of Niles, and became the bank's first president. Mau battled vice in Niles during his tenure as mayor and handpicked the idealistic John F. Calef, a progressive young man with a bent toward reform, to be his successor. Mau is shown here with 16-year-old Florence Nelson, a bank teller, after the bank was robbed in 1930. The institution became insolvent during the Great Depression and closed.

John F. Calef dramatically improved the fire department and built a new village hall at Milwaukee and Touhy Avenues, using money raised through Niles Days, an annual summer carnival. Calef brought the Cook County state's attorney in to investigate allegations of corruption and "speed traps" within his police department. The intersection is shown above during the construction phase in 1929. The fenced area is the building site of the new village hall. Calef (right), Niles's fifth mayor, is seen as a savior of Niles, rescuing the town from going the way of many vice-ridden suburbs still carrying the stigmas from Prohibition. He successfully supported new sewers, general expansion, the widening of Milwaukee Avenue, and the paving of streets. Under his leadership, the fire department became mechanized and modernized. His opponents attempted to steal the 1927 election, running grocer Joseph Jozwiak, a World War I veteran, as their candidate for mayor. When Calef lost by a suspicious seven votes, he called for a recount and won the election. He continued to fight an uphill battle against corruption within the Niles Police Department, eventually moving to Park Ridge around 1932.

Niles Days, the annual festival, began in 1925 and included a parade through Niles and the surrounding suburbs featuring elaborate floats, dancing, a picnic, and games for kids. Justice of the Peace Conrad Stoeger poses in front of the float for his real estate office on September 17, 1925, in front of St. Adalbert's Cemetery. This was the first float ever to be entered in a Niles Days Parade. Stoeger also owned the Welcome Inn Tavern in East Maine.

William Mandernack, best known as the Cook County highway policeman in the famous morgue photograph of Baby Face Nelson, served as Niles chief of police under John F. Calef and was a staunch enemy of the Oszakowski brothers. On village election day in April 1931, Mandernack was campaigning at the polls for James Cozak, a candidate for mayor, when he was knocked senseless and kidnapped by supporters of Edward O. Clark, the opposing candidate. Mandernack was found bound and gagged but otherwise unharmed in the barn of Carl Wingstrom on Milwaukee Avenue by Cook County state attorney's investigators, sent to Niles to monitor the election. Once again, Niles received national newspaper coverage. (Original artwork by Gary Halverson from the author's personal collection.)

Joe and Anna Wagner, parents of Lois Wagner Kozeny and future village clerk Frank Wagner, pose around 1940 in front of their Burgundy Inn at 7146 North Milwaukee Avenue, formerly Bierschwale's Hardware Store and later Schaul and Sons Poultry Farms store. The Wagners previously owned The White House Tavern at 7235 North Milwaukee Avenue but sold that Niles landmark to John and Maria Ladener by 1947.

In 1930, pharmacist Mark Toepel, son of Rev. Julius Toepel, pastor of St. Mathew's Lutheran Church in East Maine, bought A.P. Gronau's Niles Pharmacy, formerly the Usis Dry Goods Store, and opened Toepel's Drugs, which he operated for many years. Toepel would eventually buy one of the first houses in Grennan Heights. The neon sign was purchased at the World's Fair in 1933, around when this photograph was taken.

Niles Chief of Police Peter Oszakowski and his sergeant, Warren Guenther, would be forced to resign from the force in 1926 amid allegations that they were running a speed trap. Mayor Calef actually turned to Julius Szatkowski, the superintendent of St. Adalbert's Cemetery, as a man he trusted to serve as temporary police chief until a suitable replacement was found. While unemployed, Oszakowski joined his brothers in running their tavern, the Avenue Inn. In 1928, he was arrested for attempting to bribe federal Prohibition agents, a crime that made national news and eventually earned the former chief a prison sentence in Leavenworth. While Oszakowski was dealing with his legal problems in 1932, his brother-in-law Frank Names, a World War I veteran and hearse driver, retrieved Oszakowski's revolver from a closet in the Names bungalow on Franks Street and shot and killed his sleeping wife (Oszakowski's sister, Hattie), before turning the gun on himself. The murder-suicide shocked Niles and was one of the most well-attended funerals of the times at St. Adalbert's.

Many notable Cook County and Chicago politicians were in attendance because of Peter Oszakowski's brother, Michael (right), the political boss of Niles. Later that year, the *Tribune* reported that Michael Oszakowski was arrested by the Chicago Police Department and brought before Judge Padden for sexually assaulting a six-year-old girl. Overnight, the Oszakowskis' political power in Niles was over.

Irish gangster Roger "The Terrible" Touhy was the undisputed crime boss of Niles and the surrounding suburbs during the heyday of Prohibition. Touhy ran his high-quality beer in trucks driven by off-duty Cook County highway policemen. In 1959, just out of prison, having been framed by Capone for kidnapping, Touhy was gunned down by Capone's men on the steps of his sister's house in Chicago. Contrary to popular belief, Touhy Avenue is not named after Roger Touhy—the street's namesake is an early 19th century founder of the Rogers Park neighborhood in Chicago, Patrick L. Touhy. (Author's personal collection.)

Edward O. Clark (1931–1933), Niles's sixth village president, shown here in his retirement years, oversaw another corrupt administration. Illegal gambling took root under Clark and his successor, Michael Didier, during the 1930s. The foundation of vice laid by organized crime in Niles during these years would remain unbroken until the late 1950s. Clark lived on Oakton Street and got himself elected township highway commissioner, but in 1940, he was indicted by a grand jury for malfeasance. The indictment alleged that Clark received taxpayer money for supervising the upkeep of only 366 feet of road.

Niles was considered the gateway to "Rural Bohemia," the name given to the suburban roadhouse district of speakeasies and resorts north of Chicago by Prohibition-era newspapers. Niles was second only to neighboring Morton Grove in the number of illegal taverns within its boundaries. And there were even more hotspots north of the village on Milwaukee Avenue in Maine Township. One such establishment was the Sans Souci, a resort on Milwaukee Avenue within walking distance of the Cook County Highway Police Station. On August 9, 1929, Theodore Schuette (right), the chief of police of Elmwood Park, Illinois, was making a tour of Rural Bohemia with two female companions, and wound up intoxicated at the Sans Souci. Schuette began waving his revolver around, threatening to "shoot up the place." The bartender ran to the Cook County police station and summoned help. County policeman Fred Bryant (left) responded to the Sans Souci with his partner, and Schuette was still brandishing his revolver. Bryant's partner moved to disarm Schuette, who pushed him aside and raised his pistol. Bryant then shot Schuette four times, killing him. The Cook County policemen were exonerated by a coroner's inquest. Schuette (right) left behind a wife and five children. (Original drawings by Gary Halverson from the author's personal collection.)

During the predawn hours of December 28, 1927, Johnny Touhy, brother of Roger Touhy, entered Bob Freebus's Lone Tree Tavern at 7710 North Milwaukee Avenue, at that time just north of the village limits, with six of his henchmen to settle a score with a rival alcohol distributor. Touhy and his men began shooting, firing a total of 45 shots, seven of which hit their target, Charles Miller, an independent booze peddler, who was killed. An hour later, a dying man with a bullet in his brain was dumped in the lobby of Northwestern University Hospital in Chicago. He was initially identified as John Davis, but when Cook County police viewed the corpse later that day, they were able to positively identify him as Johnny Touhy. He had been shot and killed by his own men. These photos of the barroom were taken by a crime reporter shortly after the shooting, and doubled as both press photos and police crime scene photos. The story brought more national news attention to Niles.

On weekends, northbound traffic on Milwaukee Avenue would back up for miles through Niles and far beyond, the result of thousands of Chicagoans fleeing to the northern lakes for their days off. As early as 1900, the farmers of Maine Township formed the Anti-Auto League to discuss the problem of the invading motorcars, particularly at the intersection of Milwaukee Avenue and Dempster Street in East Maine. In 1928, construction was begun on an underpass, or viaduct, to relieve congestion on Milwaukee Avenue by having Dempster Street, the main thoroughfare to Evanston and the lakefront, run under the northbound traffic on Milwaukee Avenue. The photograph below was taken looking west from the roof of Ray Steil's house on Dempster Street at the height of construction. The large white semi-Victorian building at the southeast corner of Milwaukee Avenue and Dempster Street is Beto's Corners, with a grocery store in front and a tavern called the Welcome Inn around back. (Courtesy of Robert Steil.)

Grennan Heights, settled by Jacob Heinz in the 1800s, is the residential area most commonly associated with Niles. The streets were paved during the Depression, setting the stage for a housing boom, which was stopped by World War II but resumed shortly after. This sign from the 1930s encouraged travelers on Milwaukee Avenue to consider relocating to this "exclusive" residential community of brick residences and doublewide sidewalks. Michael Didier (right), the seventh president of Niles (1933–1941), continued the legacy of Edward Clark in looking the other way on illegal gambling. During Mayor Didier's tenure, there was a referendum to change the village's name from Niles to Grennan Heights.

Village officials, prominent citizens, and volunteer fireman posed with their brand new Pirsch Pumper, Engine No. 1, during their picnic in 1935. This fire engine was retired to Point Park in the 1960s. Mayor Michael Didier (wearing necktie) stands on the running board and trustee Frank Stankowicz is at the wheel. Police Sergeant Charles Zaleski (also wearing a necktie) is at the rear corner of the wagon, carrying the 1905 hand pump. Zaleski was involved in the shooting of a violent stalker in 1940, and left the force a short time later. Joseph Jozwiak, a mayoral candidate in 1927

and owner of a grocery store and deli, is directly opposite Zaleski at the back of the cart. Jozwiak would be elected police magistrate the following year and be reelected for four consecutive terms, hearing an estimated 20,000 cases in his time on the bench. Jozwiak, a World War I veteran, was not a lawyer and had no formal legal training; he studied law books and interviewed attorneys to prepare himself for his run for magistrate. (Author's personal collection.)

Members of the Niles Volunteer Fire Company pose with Chief George Pasek (center, in white shirt) at the Marvel Picnic Grove during their annual picnic in 1935. August Kadlec, looking elderly but robust, is to Chief Pasek's right. At this time, Kadlec had served more than 35 years with the volunteer fire company. Leroy "Skid" Prideux, the custodian and caretaker of the Cook County Highway Police Station for more than 30 years, lies down between the two rows. Prideux lived with his wife on the third floor of the station. He was best known for erecting a large, fully lit Christmas tree in the cupola of the police station every holiday season.

All roads seemed to end in Niles during Prohibition. In this photograph from September 25, 1930, Chicago police lieutenant Andrew Barry interviews mob gun-runner Willie Jackson at the Cook County sheriff's police station after Jackson's arrest in Niles. Jackson was alleged to have supplied the "Tommy-guns" used in the St. Valentine's Day Massacre of 1929, in which seven of Bugs Moran's gangsters were brutally murdered by Al Capone's hit men posing as police officers. (Author's personal collection.)

On October 28, 1936, two hit men walked into Charlotte's Cocktail Lounge at 7225 North Milwaukee Avenue and announced a robbery. The manager and house bookie, 32-year-old Adolph Anzona (right), was playing pinochle with the bartender and the cook in the dining room. Anzona knew it was no robbery and quickly sought cover, but to no avail. He was killed by shots from a sawed-off shotgun and a semi-automatic pistol. It was later theorized that the killing was payback because Anzona had been the chauffeur of gangster Jack Klutas, and was believed to have set his boss up to be arrested. Klutas refused to be taken alive and was killed in a 1933 shootout with police in Bellwood, Illinois. Below, Bill Mehring's Lounge, shown on the right around 1960, had not changed much since it was Charlotte's Cocktail Lounge in 1936, site of the Anzona slaying. (Original drawing by Russ McAndrew from the author's personal collection.)

The abandoned caretaker's house at the Bunker Hill Forest Preserve on Harts Road is believed to have been Elmer Getty's Atlasta Farm Recreation Club, aka the "Alaska Club," a private speakeasy that catered to an exclusive clientele, which according to Justice Department transcripts included John Dillinger and Lester Gillis, aka George "Baby Face" Nelson. In 1932, five gangsters went to the club to kill Getty, who wasn't there. Elmer Russell, a 40-year-old waiter, was asked his name by the gunmen and was only able to speak his first name, Elmer, before being killed by the gunmen, a victim of mistaken identity.

The Avenue Inn, aka "Mike's Place," owned by bootlegger and accused child-rapist Michael Oszakowski, was located one door south of the Silver Leaf Tavern and stood on the southern portion of today's White Eagle. In 1929, the speakeasy was fire-bombed by a rival faction operating out of the Radio Club, an Italian-run saloon nearby on Milwaukee Avenue. The vacant Avenue Inn is shown here in the 1930s prior to being razed.

The Silver Leaf Tavern, seen here in the 1930s, was later sold and renamed the House of Tromba in the 1940s, and later the White Eagle. Michael Nowakowski, the owner of the Silver Leaf in the 1930s, was arrested several times for running an illegal slot machine parlor after numerous raids by the Cook County state's attorney and highway police.

In 1921, Al Maitzen opened his Ideal Overall Service, later changed to Ideal Uniform Rental Service, at 7241 North Waukegan Road in this beautiful, slate-roofed gothic structure, shown here in 1936. The business specialized in providing clean coveralls to factories and plants around Chicago, including pickup and drop-off laundry service. Ideal Uniform, which closed and was torn down in the 1990s, was the first of many industrial companies to make Niles home from the 1920s through the 1950s.

Robert Romey was appointed chief of police in 1936 and served continuously until retiring in 1961. Tam O'Shanter Country Club owner George S. May made Romey his chief of security, a job Romey performed in addition to his police chief duties for decades. In April 1937, Romey's sergeant, Charles Zaleski, was summoned to a disturbance at 7124 North Milwaukee Avenue, where 21-year-old Chicagoan Willard Schultz had just choked and beaten his ex-girlfriend, Dolores Tamillo, 19, and her friend, Leonard Nowakowski, who had come to her aid. As Sergeant Zaleski pulled up, Schultz, in a jealous rage, fled in a car, kicking off a high-speed chase southbound on Milwaukee Avenue. Schultz bailed out of his vehicle at 5534 North Elston Avenue in Chicago and began to run. Zaleski fired a warning shot, and then fired again, striking Schultz in the back of the head and killing him. Zaleski was cleared of any wrongdoing by a coroner's inquest, at which Schultz's mother forgave Zaleski. Sergeant Zaleski left the force a short time later. Officer Leonard Krysiak (below), poses on his motorcycle in 1935, when Niles policemen were still part-time, hourly employees of the village, with no pension or benefits. (Courtesy of Lois Kozeny.)

Six

TRUCK FARMING
A WAY OF LIFE

The truck farmers of Niles and Maine Townships were mostly Lutherans, and overwhelmingly German. The notable exception was an Italian named Jonathan Vinci, who was still farming the northeast corner of Milwaukee Avenue and Golf Road in the early 1970s. The transition was eventually made from horse-drawn farm implements to motorized tractors, but the premise remained the same: farm well-organized tracts of vegetables, and truck them to wholesale markets in Chicago. The farming families of Niles and East Maine read their Bibles and attended church regularly, kept their amusements clean (for the most part), and valued their families and neighbors as much as they valued honesty and hard work—these things meant the world to them. Ray Steil and his father John are shown above with their remaining draft horses, the last vestiges of the 19th century way of farming. (Courtesy of Robert Steil.)

Ray Steil's grandfather Dietrich Steil (1840–1924), shown here in the yard of his home at 7850 West Dempster Street in what would eventually become Niles, claimed that he could read a book by the light of the Great Chicago Fire in the summer of 1871, while sitting in this very same chair. The Steils immigrated from Germany in the mid-1800s and still own the piece of property Dietrich Steil is sitting on in this photograph from around 1890. He is buried in St. Mathew's Cemetery. (Courtesy of Robert Steil.)

Four-year-old Ray Steil (1914–2011) plays with his collie Buster in front of his father's house at 7850 West Dempster Street. The house still stands and is owned by Ray's son, Robert. The 60 acres of onions, tomatoes, and sugar beets are long gone—Ray stopped farming in 1961. Farming was a way of life, and boys started helping their fathers at a young age. The Steils and other families like them raised vegetables and transported them to the Randolph Street Wholesale Market in Chicago. (Courtesy of Robert Steil.)

The farming families of eastern Maine Township, or "East Maine," as the area from north of Oakton Street to what is now Golf Road was known, centered their lives around their church. St. Mathew's Lutheran Church, seen here, was founded in the late 1800s on land donated by the Jaacks family. The original church, an offshoot of St. John's to the south, was torn down in the 1980s, but the parsonage still stands.

The truck farmers living north of Niles preferred to conduct all of their business outside the village. The farmer's Savings and Loan pictured here was located on Milwaukee Avenue near Golf Road, although its exact location is lost to history.

John Beto and his family operated this store, tavern, and meeting hall on the southeast corner of Milwaukee Avenue and Dempster Street from the late 1800s until the 1920s. Shown above in 1900, the front part of the large building was a grocery store called Beto's Corners, and the back of the building housed the tavern and hall, known as The Welcome Inn. Below, John Beto poses with his delivery wagon.

John Jaacks, shown in front of his roadside stand on Milwaukee Avenue, immigrated to the United States from Holstein, Germany, to become a prosperous farmer in East Maine. He was a Cook County highway commissioner in 1914 and, as president of the commission, was instrumental in paving many streets in Maine and Niles Townships. Jaacks was also a charter member of the Cook County Truck Gardeners and Farmers Association. The Jaacks family market (below) sold everything from turkey, geese, and duck to fresh fruits and vegetables in the 1940s.

The Schuemann family farm on the east side of Milwaukee Avenue at Crain Street is now occupied by a Polish deli and Grendel's Oil Change Shop. Patrons of the picnic grove across the street from the farm would sneak onto the Schuemann property to use their outhouse. The Schaefer farm (below) was located approximately where the main gate for Maryhill Cemetery is located today. The Schaefers' neighbors to the west were the Ellerbrocks, who lived in the house that became the Maryhill caretaker's house in the 1950s. The Ellerbrocks farmed the land that today comprises the western part of the cemetery off of Cumberland and the Greenwood Estates subdivision.

The East Maine School was just south of Holsum Bread on Milwaukee Avenue, where Doerner Jewelers stood before it was razed. Later, the school moved to the current Northridge Prep building. Here, the students pose with their teacher, possibly Miss Egan, around 1920.

The Loeding family farm stood on the south side of Dempster, on what is now Notre Dame High School property. Pictured here in 1910, from left to right, are Amanda Schubert, Gus Loeding Jr., Ida Loeding, Alma Loeding Stanke, Gus Loeding Sr., Herman Loeding, and Ernest Loeding. The Loedings also owned a farm on the north side of Dempster near the Schroeder Nursery in today's Morton Grove.

Ray Steil was 15 years old and attending Maine Township High School—later Maine East—when he drove this brand-new 1929 Ford Model A to school. One of his favorite amusements was paying 5¢ to drive it on the "Whoopie Coaster," a traveling Depression-era wooden rollercoaster that was built to accommodate motorcars. The Whoopie Coaster in Niles was identical to the one below and was located at 9055 North Milwaukee Avenue where Sullivan's Tavern once stood. (Above, courtesy of Robert Steil; below, courtesy of Los Angeles Public Library.)

There were several horrible auto accidents during the Depression. The Hi-Way Truck Stop and Auto Wreckers at Milwaukee Avenue and Ballard Road is shown in these two images from the 1930s. There were no expressways, so there was always heavy truck traffic on Milwaukee Avenue, including truck farmers from north of East Maine and Niles bringing their vegetable crops to market in Chicago.

Henry A. Joern, a farmer and contractor, rides horseback with his daughter, Vera, on his farmstead at 8500 North Cumberland Avenue in the 1940s. The land across Cumberland Avenue is adjacent to the Dempster Golf Club, which occupied the northwest quadrant of today's Maryhill Cemetery property. Henry Joern's horses (below) graze in the foreground across from the Cumberland Avenue entrance to the Dempster Golf Club in the 1940s. (Courtesy of Tina Joern.)

Little Annie Shroeder and her younger brother Albert tend to chickens at the Shroeder farm on Harts and Gross Point Roads and Touhy and Caldwell Avenues around 1900. Below, from left to right, Carl Schroeder, Sophia Topp Schroeder, and their sons, William and Albert, pose in front of the farmhouse around 1918.

John Steil and Frieda Schuemann pose on their wedding day in 1910. John built the house at 7850 West Dempster Street for his new bride as a wedding present and it is still in the family. The Steils employed a regular crew of seasonal migrant workers, Mexicans who would make the long trek up through Texas to work on midwestern farms in the summer. During World War II, German POWs from Camp Pine in Mount Prospect were paroled to work on the Steil farm as well. The German POWs probably felt at home with the farmers of East Maine, who were of predominantly German descent and often still spoke German in their homes. (Courtesy of Robert Steil.)

A crowd looks on as the newly-paved Milwaukee Avenue is dedicated on April 22, 1915. The man wearing overalls at the far right is August Geweke (1862–1945), president of the Cook County Truck Farmer's Association, which as an affiliate of the Associated Roads Organization of Chicago and Cook County, did most of the legwork to get the improvements done in Niles. Geweke's father farmed the land at the southwest corner of Harlem Avenue and Dempster Street, which August inherited. August Geweke was known as the "Pickle King" of East Maine, due to his most prominent crop.

John Steil poses with his son, Ray, and their canine companion with a truckload of pumpkins in the 1940s. Illinois was and still is the largest producer of pumpkins in the country. Ray Steil and his wife, Loretta Grewe Steil (below), married in 1937. She was the love of his life, and preceded him in death in 1998. Their first date was at the Niles Inn, formerly Niemann's Place. Their only child, Robert, or Bob, was born in 1950. Like many of the truck farmers in Niles, the Steils began selling off their land to developers during the housing boom of the 1950s. Ray Steil stopped farming in Niles in 1961, but maintained an interest in a dairy farm in Harvard, Illinois, until his death in 2011 at the age of 97.

Bob Steil stands in his father's onion field near Dempster Street and Ozanam Avenue in 1955. Within a few years of this photograph, Ray built a baseball diamond in this field for Bob and his friends, even erecting a light pole in the field so the boys could play after dark. Bob remembers that no matter how early his father had woken up on any given day, and no matter how tired he was from working in the fields, he never said no when Bob and his friends asked him to pitch to them on the baseball diamond.

Ray was a staunch Chicago Cubs fan until the day he died, and would often take Bob to Wrigley Field at the spur of the moment, buying tickets at the gate for that day's game.

Seven

SPORTS AND RECREATION

John F. Calef loved baseball, and he formed the Niles Athletic Club (NAC) baseball team before World War I so that he and his teammates could play the game whenever possible. The NAC practiced and played home games in a field that would become Jozwiak Park almost 50 years later. The club competed against teams from neighboring suburbs, as well as barnstorming and Negro League organizations. The Niles Tigers organized in the 1920s, to serve the needs of players age 16 and under, but were affiliated with the village of Niles in name only, as they were private clubs. Little League did not come to Niles until the 1950s. Niles officially voted to organize a park district in 1954.

John F. Calef poses in his Niles Athletic Club uniform around 1915, in the field that eventually became Jozwiak Park, and which currently houses the Niles Public Works complex. Calef, a lifelong baseball fan, attended Chicago Cubs and Chicago Whales games every chance he got. Many members of the NAC were also members of the volunteer fire company. The NAC stayed active into the 1930s; by then, players 16 and over played on the NAC, while younger players joined the Niles Tigers. Below, Joe and Frank Wagner goof around in their pinstriped Niles Tigers uniforms in 1926 behind their parents' tavern, the Niles White House on Milwaukee Avenue.

Joe Wagner, owner of the White House and later the Burgundy Inn, wearing the uniform of the Niles Athletic Club, holds his daughter Lois in the late 1930s. Wagner was drafted into the US Navy in World War II, when he was in his 40s. Below, the pugnacious Cook County Highway Police softball team poses behind their police station in 1936 with their batboys. Sgt. Jimmy Allegretti, a decorated officer who fought organized crime throughout the 1930s, is seated second from left in the second row.

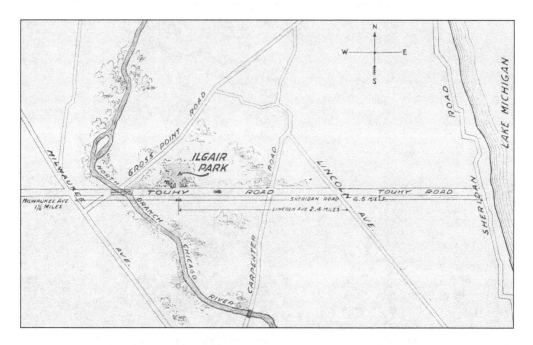

In 1932, wealthy inventor and industrialist Robert Alexander Ilg (1879–1964) established Ilgair Park, a privately owned resort and recreation area, at 6300 West Touhy Avenue—the current home of the YMCA—to serve as a weekend getaway for his employees and their families. Eventually, Ilg opened the park to outside groups as well. He constructed a half-sized reproduction of the Leaning Tower of Pisa (below) on the grounds of Ilgair Park, to be used as a water tower and pumping station. It supplied spring water to Lake Caldwell and a large outdoor swimming pool. When the tower was completed, Ilg dedicated it to the memory of Galileo.

G.1152—Chicagoland's "Leaning Tower of Pisa"

Where Nature Welcomes You Royally-

ILGAIR PARK

Amidst its tree-lined walkways, Ilgair Park featured a windmill and observation tower as well as Lake Caldwell, a small, manmade lake complete with a miniature island and artistic footbridges. There was also an outdoor swimming pool and "diving tower." Ilg claimed that the 40-foot-by-75-foot pool was the largest in Illinois. The pool featured an underground tunnel around its perimeter where spectators could watch swimmers underwater through lighted portholes. There was a Moorish-style pavilion or "Colonnade" at the north end of the pool and a similarly designed field house to the east. (Courtesy of Russ McAndrew.)

The 1933–1934 Niles Elementary School boys basketball team poses above at the back of the school, in front of the coal door. This view looks east toward the field that would later become Jozwiak Park. The wooden apparatus in the far background may be the backstop used by the Niles Athletic Club on their baseball diamond. Basketball was a very popular interleague sport at Niles Elementary in the 1930s. Below, the girls team poses in the same location with the coach they shared with the boys team.

Dam No. 2 of the Cook County Forest Preserves, located off of River Road just north of Des Plaines, was a wildly popular recreation site for Niles residents in the 1920s and 1930s. The above image shows the Dam in July 1927, with some children fully clothed in the Des Plaines River. The giant water slide, known as the "Miniature Shoot-the-Chutes," was gone by 1932, when the below photograph was taken. Cars could drive across the river amid the flowing waters of the dam. Dam No. 2 was also the site of an annual water carnival and canoe marathon. (Both, author's personal collection.)

Annette Rogers Kelly (1913–2006) won gold medals in the 4-by-100-meter relay at the 1932 Olympics in Los Angeles and the 1936 Olympics in Berlin. Kelly settled in Niles after World War II, and at the time of her death in 2006, was a member of the St. John Brebeuf Roman Catholic Parish. At the 1936 Berlin Olympics, Kelly and other American gold medalists had to cup their medals in their hands in order to hide them. They were instructed by their Nazi hosts to do so because Hitler was furious over the American victories and did not want to see their gold medals at the closing ceremony. Kelly is seen here with her 1936 relay teammates. (Author's personal collection.)

Mayor Frank Stankowicz (right) confers with future director of public works Ed Bacher (left) during the construction of Niles Park on Touhy Avenue in 1951. The village took over the field just east of the public school to create a public park. The Niles Athletic Club had been playing baseball games in the field since before World War I.

Chester "Chet" Hajduk (1919–2006) signed with the Chicago White Sox in 1940 and played Class C ball with their minor league team in Lubbock, Texas. Hajduk led his league in batting, and was brought up to the majors to play for the White Sox in 1941, but his one professional season was cut short when he broke his arm playing first base. He was back with the White Sox for spring training in 1942, but promptly joined the US Navy during World War II. Hajduk played for the Great Lakes naval base team after joining the service and was moved up to the Armed Services All-Star team due to his hot bat. It was on this team that he played against Joe Dimaggio and Ted Williams. Hajduk settled in Niles after World War II, becoming a successful building contractor and raising his family. (Author's personal collection.)

The Bunker Hill Country Club, Niles's "other" golf club, was located at 6635 North Milwaukee Avenue and had 18 holes with rolling, forested greens. The above image shows the course during its development period in the 1920s. The club was plagued by financial troubles over the years and suffered a damaging fire in the 1940s. Forced to sell off its land to the Cook County Forest Preserve to stay afloat, the golf course was eventually closed in the 1950s, becoming a VFW Post with a popular restaurant and banquet hall open to the public. Below, caddies Jon Oxley and Peter Sklar wade through the flooded fifth hole after a record-breaking rainstorm on September 14, 1936. (Below, author's personal collection.)

Eight

THE TAM O'SHANTER
COUNTRY CLUB

The Tam O'Shanter Country Club opened in the 1920s at Howard Street and Caldwell Road, on land formerly occupied by Peter Thorsen's brickyard, which supplied the bricks for almost every masonry building built in the formative years of Niles. "The Tam" was a popular but unassuming country club until George S. May (1890–1962), known as the "P.T. Barnum of Golf," bought the club in the late 1930s. May was the first course owner to offer substantial cash prizes to the winners of his tournaments, the first to allow the use of golf carts, the first to televise a professional golfing event, the first to install grandstands for spectators, and the first to use radios to keep spectators informed of the action on the greens. His antics even earned him a full profile in the August 1, 1955, issue of the fledgling *Sports Illustrated*, then only a year old. The original clubhouse is pictured in this 1930s postcard. (Author's personal collection.)

This advertisement for Tam O'Shanter as a party venue promotes the club's "year-round enjoyment."

This historical postcard shows the new clubhouse that served as the backdrop to Tam's heyday. This building would burn in 1946, but was rebuilt. Between 1940 and 1965, nearly every professional golfer of consequence, both male and female, competed at Tam. May, who was a personal friend of boxer and avid golfer Joe Louis, was also the first promoter to integrate his tournaments and welcome qualified African American golfers to the professional circuit. (Author's personal collection.)

G.1151—Tam O' Shanter Country Club, Show Place of Chicagoland

George S. May poses with two models and a pile of cash in this publicity photo for his All-American Golf Tournament in 1945. The contest offered $60,000 in matured value war bonds for prizes. In July 1953, May's World Championship of Golf became the first professional golf tournament to be shown on national television. The American Broadcasting Company (ABC), new to the medium of television, saw the value of televising the event because the $25,000 prize was higher than any other payout in the sport. They charged May $32,000 to cover the final hour of the tournament and May paid up. A single television camera was mounted on top of the grandstand overlooking the 18th hole. In the last 10 minutes of the live broadcast, Lew Worsham, the pro at Oakmont Country Club outside of Pittsburgh, trailing by a stroke, made an unbelievable 115-yard eagle to win the tournament and take home the $25,000. One million viewers watched on television in what may have been May's finest hour.

George and Dorothy May dressed up for this formal occasion at "The Tam." The club hosted weddings, proms, college formals, Bar Mitzvahs, political events, and birthday parties.

Niles volunteer firefighters fight an early morning blaze in the clubhouse at the Tam O'Shanter Country Club on September 21, 1946. While no one was injured in the fire, damages were estimated at up to $300,000. (Author's personal collection.)

Bing Crosby and Bob Hope performed their comedy routine on the 17th hole at Tam O'Shanter after playing a charity round in May 1945. It was the most well-attended event in the course's history. In an unusually cold spring, thousands turned out, and many even climbed trees to watch the two celebrities. (Author's personal collection.)

Niles police investigate the wreckage of a privately-owned BT-13 Navy trainer airplane that crashed into a steel fence near the 15th green about 100 feet from Caldwell Road on September 15, 1946. The pilot and owner, Chicago radio announcer John Neblett, and his passenger, Bruce Buckingham, were both killed. The two had taken off from Palwaukee Airport in Wheeling, and, ironically, had played a round of golf at Tam earlier that day. (Author's personal collection.)

"The Brown Bomber" Joe Lewis, heavyweight boxing champ, US Army sergeant, and scratch golfer, walked the course at Tam with a group of excited young caddies in July 1943, during World

War II. George S. May was adamant that anyone who could qualify for his tournaments would be allowed to play, and insisted that his course remain integrated. (Author's personal collection.)

For all its accomplishments, Tam O'Shanter Country Club did have a dark side. Al Capone's Chicago Outfit operated a full-service, illegal casino in the basement of the club, under the supervision of Capone's financial advisor and political fixer, Jake "Greasy Thumb" Guzik (left), a frequent visitor at Tam. Slot machines were supplied exclusively by Edward "Dutch" Vogel, the mob's elusive "slot king." Vogel facilitated the Torrio-Capone organization's entrance into Cicero to help fix the elections of 1924. He also owned Apex Amusement Company, which moved from Lincoln Avenue in Chicago to Milwaukee Avenue in Niles. (Both author's personal collection.)

On July 4, 1950, during a fireworks display, the illegal casino at Tam was raided by the Cook County state's attorney's office and an unsuspecting May was arrested in front of the crowd. May was subpoenaed to testify in front of the Kefauver Hearings on Organized Crime, but pleaded the Fifth Amendment on nearly every question he was asked. He would later state publicly that he was in fear for his life. May is shown leaving the hearings at the Chicago Palmer House, looking somewhat shaken. (Author's personal collection.)

Sgt. Joseph Carroll and detective Martin Maher, assigned to the Cook County state's attorney, confiscate the roulette wheel at Tam during the raid. (Author's personal collection.)

Niles police chief Robert Romey (far left) escorts professional golfer and Niles resident Lloyd Mangrum and his wife on the platform at Chicago's Union Station. Mangrum had just returned to Illinois after winning the St. Paul Tournament, and had received an anonymous phone call threatening him with death if he won. Golf great Sam Snead also received a death threat. It is believed that illegal sports books taking action on professional golf were the cause of the threats. Below, Mangrum competes at Tam later in the season, while guarded by Romey and a squad of uniformed police officers. (Both, author's personal collection.)

Pro Lew Worsham's amazing 115-yard eagle shot for victory at the 1953 World Championship of Golf is recreated in this historical postcard. One million television viewers tuned in to ABC to watch Worsham take home the $25,000 prize. (Author's personal collection.)

255—Lew Worsham at
Tam O'Shanter Country Club

Babe Zaharias, one of the finest female golfers of all time, kisses her putter after winning the Women's All-American Golf Tournament at Tam O'Shanter Country Club on August 6, 1950. Zaharias won with a record-breaking eight-under-par score of 296. She had recently been named "Woman Athlete of the Half-Century." The previous week, Zaharias, 35, shot a 70 in the opening round, setting a course record at Tam. (Author's personal collection.)

In these promotional photos from the 1940s, George S. May poses with his young general manager, Herbert Koepke, in front of an elaborate cake decorated to look like the clubhouse. Below, May and Koepke look over the flooded course. This was a semi-regular occurrence, when the north branch of the Chicago River overflowed its banks. Tam O'Shanter offered its members a trap-skeet shooting range during the offseason months in lieu of golf.

Sam Snead putts the 18th green at the World Golf Tournament at Tam on August 14, 1949. He finished with a 68 for the day, one stroke behind the leaders going into the final round. Large crowds were the norm at Tam. In this image, one of George S. May's signature grandstands is visible, as is the landmark "golf ball" water tower. The farms across Caldwell Avenue in the background sit on land that later housed an industrial park featuring the Salerno McGowan Biscuit Company. (Author's personal collection.)

The caddy shack at Tam O'Shanter was top notch; May built this private club within the club for his caddies at a cost of $22,500. Shown here on July 15, 1955, the shack had its own dining room and commissary, a television and radio, plus a basketball court, bike rack, and telephones. (Author's personal collection.)

The cameras were rolling when Henry Ransom teed off to begin his final 18 holes at the World Tournament on August 13, 1949. The winner would take home a cool $11,000. Ransom and Chick Harbert competed for the lead on this final day of play. Anticipating the future, George S. May warned ticket holders at the World Championship of Golf in 1949 that they might be on television. Following May's historic television broadcast in 1953, the US Open was televised for the first time in 1954, and the Masters in 1956. (Both, author's personal collection.)

Nine

WORLD WAR II AND THE WINDS OF CHANGE

After World War II, many venerable Niles institutions, such as the Niles Inn, formerly Niemann's Place, changed to adapt to the times. The new owner of this Niles landmark changed it to a hotel/motel to accommodate the increased travel to Niles during the postwar years. Charles Carlino continued to operate a tavern in the basement of the building, calling it the "Cellar Club." (Author's personal collection.)

Frank J. Stankowicz was elected the eighth village president (mayor) in 1941, and served five consecutive terms until being voted out of office in 1961. Stankowicz was instrumental in setting the stage for Niles to become a modern, fully developed suburb. He encouraged residential and industrial development and modernized the police, fire, and public works departments. In 1953, a special census determined that Niles had tripled in size within three and a half years, going from 3,587 residents in 1950 to 6,883 in September 1953. This was only the beginning; the boom was far from over. In 1955, the village board voted to modernize the water supply system. The existing reservoir at Touhy and Harlem Avenues was expanded, an elevated storage tank was added on Oriole Street, and a new 16-inch supply main was installed, increasing water pressure and connecting Niles to the Mayfair pumping station in Chicago. The 1950s saw unprecedented residential expansion and population growth in Niles and the baby boom eventually added thousands of students to the school system, Soon, the Niles Public School was not enough to handle the population explosion. New schools needed to be built and teachers needed to be hired to staff them. The future was coming to Niles at a rapid pace. Stankowicz remained popular with his constituents throughout the 1950s, even in the face of outside criticism that he was soft on illegal gambling.

Lester Laid is shown here with Chief Deputy Bailiff Joseph Lelivelt after surrendering himself to the Grand Jury on October 9, 1942, for questioning about illegal gambling in his jurisdiction. Laid was in command of the Cook County Sheriff's Highway Police Station on Milwaukee Avenue throughout Prohibition and its aftermath. As a lieutenant, he often accompanied Niles police officers, including Chief Pete Oszakowski, on selected raids throughout Niles and Maine Townships. Oszakowski even worked for Laird as a highway policeman after serving his federal prison sentence for bribery. In 1942, Laird was forced to resign his position as chief of the Highway Police when he was caught having dinner at the Drake Hotel with William "Billy" Skidmore, the Chicago Outfit's "number one gambling fixer." (Author's personal collection.)

In 1939, the first Niles Township High School was opened in Niles Centre (later Skokie) to serve the residents of Niles for the first time. Up until this school opened, Niles students were required to attend private high schools or public schools in Chicago, like Schurz. Maine Township High School served residents in that township. The new Niles school is shown when it first opened its doors. (Author's personal collection.)

Niles Food Shop , a grocery store and deli at 6881 North Milwaukee Avenue, was owned by Judge Joseph Jozwiak, a self-taught justice of the peace who served five terms as police magistrate. Jozwiak's store later became Pock's, and is currently The Chambers Restaurant.

Jozwiak (seen during retirement) was a World War I veteran who was very active in the VFW post at Bunker Hill later in life. Judge Jozwiak heard an estimated 20,000 cases in 20 years on the bench before retiring in 1955. Notably, he ruled to suppress evidence taken in a raid on illegal gambling at Tam O'Shanter Country Club in the 1940s.

Leonard Schiller (on tricycle) and his cousins hang out in front of the Little Palmer House tavern on Albion Street in the late 1940s. This tavern was a favorite of retired Niles police captain Andy Cameron, who lived nearby. The Schillers lived above the Nosal Brothers Market, next to the bar. Leonard is the nephew of St. Adalbert's former superintendent, the late Julius Szatkowski. The interior of Al Schlau's Wooden Shoe Restaurant at 8100 North Caldwell Avenue is seen below in 1948, featuring an early shuffleboard machine. Pinball machines were banned in Niles in 1961 due to the propensity for people to bet on the games. (Above, courtesy of Leonard Schiller.)

At some point in the 1940s, Xavier Wojtkiewicz, the official grave decorator at St. Adalbert's Cemetery, moved his flower and garden greenhouse operation from Milwaukee Avenue to this location on Touhy Avenue across from the Niles Public School. When Wojtkiewicz died, the business was run by his children and son-in-law. (Both, courtesy of Leonard Schiller.)

Xavier Wojtkiewicz's son, Ted, fought the Japanese in the Pacific in some of the bloodiest combat of World War II. The young Marine returned home to Niles, and lived a quiet bachelor's life on Waukegan Road, never speaking about his experiences in the war. Some of his closest friends had no idea what he had been through. Wojtkiewicz, now employed by Skokie Public Works, found comfort in baseball, becoming a winning little league coach in Niles. When he was not coaching baseball, the reluctant hero could be found in the stands at Jozwiak Park, watching baseball for hours on end and barely saying a word. (Courtesy of Leonard Schiller.)

War Bond drives were very popular in Niles during World War II. Ed Bacher (the fireman third from left), was instrumental in establishing the Niles park district in 1954, and would serve as the director of public works for many years. Niles police magistrate Anton Smigiel, successor to Judge Jozwiak, is at the far right.

Chief George Pasek inspects Niles's first ambulance with other firemen in 1948. A firehouse and garage were added to the village hall and police department during the 1940s, with the firefighters doing most of the construction work themselves at no cost to the village. Pasek was appointed to the Niles Volunteer Fire Company on May 1, 1934. He became its chief on May 19, 1936. The following year, Pasek became the paid fire chief for the Village of Niles at a salary of $5 per month. Chief Pasek was an engineer with extensive technical knowledge. In addition to making the Niles Fire Department a model agency with national recognition, he also designed the mechanical gates at St. Adalbert's Cemetery. Niles ambulance service predates the Chicago Fire Department's program. Niles's first ambulance was purchased for $6,000 after a door-to-door fundraising campaign overseen by Chief Pasek. He retired in 1964. (Author's personal collection.)

The entire Niles Fire Department poses with their equipment—including "Blue Boy," their original hand-pumper—on the driveway of the village hall in 1948. In the 1950s, the fire department moved towards establishing a full-time department for the first time in the history of Niles.

This aerial view of the eastern portion of Niles from around 1950 shows Caldwell Avenue running in a curved line at the bottom and the intersection of Oakton Street and Waukegan Road at the upper left. Oscar Franson's farm is clearly visible at the northeast corner of this intersection. The open land to the extreme right later became Lawrencewood Shopping Center. Abandoned farms such as the old Krueger place on Oakton (below) became more and more common in the 1950s, as farms were replaced by tract homes.

Shown at the police station on Milwaukee Avenue on June 27, 1952, Sheriff John Babb (left) inventories illegal slot machines taken in raids by his officers. The new decade ushered in increased intolerance for organized crime and illegal gambling from the Cook County state's attorney and sheriff's police. A war on slots was waged in taverns across the suburbs, and Niles was ground zero. When a whistle-blower alleged to the *Chicago Tribune* that Niles was the mob's headquarters for illegal slot machine operations, Cook County law enforcement cracked down. (Author's personal collection.)

Sheriff John Babb spoke to a gathering of local police chiefs, including Niles Police Chief Robert Romey, at the Bunker Hill Country Club in Niles in 1952. The topics of discussion included modern methods of policing, ethics in law enforcement, and professionalizing police departments. (Author's personal collection.)

JOKER JOE'S TYPHOON CLUB
7052 Milwaukee Avenue
Niles, Illinois

Eccentric saloonkeeper Joe Siciliani operated "Joker Joe's Typhoon Club" in Niles from the 1940s until the late 1960s. Although it had a bad reputation with reform-minded politicians looking for a scapegoat in the 1960s, Joker Joe's was known as a fun place to let loose by many people who went there. Joe's open lewdness and blue sense of humor made his place a tourist attraction for thrill-seekers who wanted to experience a dirty joke firsthand. Upon entering the front door, women were treated to a blast of compressed air from a floor grate ala Marilyn Monroe. There were also audio speakers in the ladies room. The interior of the club is shown in the historical postcard above and Joker Joe's sense of humor is best illustrated by the group of souvenirs below. (Both, author's personal collection.)

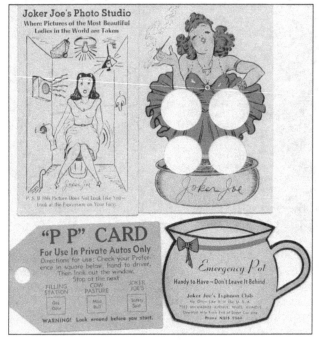

Mayor Frank Stankowicz poses with his full-time police department around 1950 (above). After World War II, the Niles Police Department was reorganized into a full-time, 24-hour police department. Below, the officers pose with their squad cars.

Monsignor Rusch of St. Hedwig's envisioned a "home, not an institution," when he laid out his plans for St. Andrew's Catholic Home for the Aged adjacent to St. Hedwig's at 7000 North Newark Avenue. World War II delayed construction until 1949, and the new home (above) was consecrated by Samuel Cardinal Stritch (left) on May 30, 1952. Monsignor Rusch celebrated the dedication Mass. At left, Cardinal Stritch gives his blessing to Mary Driscoll, 92, the oldest resident of the home. (Left, author's personal collection.)

The A.B. Dick Company, named for founder Albert Blake Dick, was an industrial printing company that perfected the process of mimeograph duplication using patents filed by Thomas Alva Edison. In 1949, the company relocated to a new plant at 5700 West Touhy Avenue, with a water tower to enhance fire protection capabilities (right). A.B. Dick also made donations to the fire department to assist with the modernization of firefighting equipment. More industry would move to Niles during this period, including The Teletype Corporation and the Salerno McGowan Biscuit Company. An industrial tax base was created and the groundwork was being laid for the expansion and further development of the village of Niles. (Both, author's personal collection.)

Judge Anton Andrew Smigiel (1911–1989) grew up in Chicago, graduated from the Kent College of Law in 1942, and was admitted to the Illinois Bar that same year. In 1949, he was retained by a conglomerate of 43 Niles families who had been swindled out of their money with a house-building scam that conman Robert Reed ran on Kirk Lane in Niles. Reed absconded to California but was arrested. Due to the efforts of Smigiel, the victims recovered most of their lost investments. Smigiel moved to Niles in 1942 and was active in many civic endeavors. He was elected police magistrate in 1956, and in 1960, became a judge in the third district of the Cook County Municipal Court System. Judge Smigiel lost his first wife, Sally Karwoska Smigiel, in a plane crash on February 12, 1963.

Chief Robert Romey (far right) congratulates his police officers for their victory over the fire department in a fire hose tug-of-war competition at a Niles Days Celebration in the mid-1950s. Ed Denis (next to Romey) and Bill "Whitey" Mehring (third from left, in back) both retired from the police department as captains after long and rewarding careers.

Ed Bacher and his crew take a break during the construction of Niles Park—later Jozwiak Park—in 1951. In 1952, residents helped erect the Grennan Heights Fieldhouse and Playground at Oketo Avenue and Monroe Street. In 1954, Niles passed a referendum to form a park district.

The new exit ramp to Caldwell Avenue off the Edens Expressway did not start the mass exodus of Chicagoans to new lives in the suburbs, but it assisted it greatly. Here, a young boy on the Chicago side watches the ramp on its opening day in 1955.

One last look back on the way we were: On June 6, 1930, two armed robbers entered the Niles State Bank at Milwaukee and Touhy and announced a hold-up. Theodore Kolb, 76, the Niles village treasurer, had just deposited $3,000 and his hearing loss almost cost him his life when he failed to put his hands up. The bandits relented from locking everyone in the vault because 16-year-old teller Florence Nelson was "too pretty to die of suffocation." Now, over 80 years later, it is likely that everyone in this photograph, taken the day of the robbery, is deceased. Even the jauntily-posed boy in the doorway has likely left this earth; although his name is lost to history, hopefully he lived a long, happy life—maybe he even stayed in Niles. The posters on the shed next door announce that the circus was coming to town, and that movie star cowboy Tom Mix would appear in person! Hopefully, the boy got to see Tom Mix, and one day he got to tell his grandchildren about it.

BIBLIOGRAPHY

Andreas, A.T. *History of Cook County, Illinois: From the Earliest Period to the Present Time.* Chicago: A.T. Andreas, 1884.

Bestman, James F. *The Descendants of Marx Hinrich Jaacks & Margaretha Christina Kruse, et al, From Wahlstedt, Holstein, Germany.* Addison, IL: James F. Bestman, 2004.

The Chicago Tribune (archives). Chicago: Tribune Company, 1847–1955.

The Cook County Herald (archives). Arlington Heights, IL: Paddock Publications, 1871–1955.

Goodspeed, Weston Arthur. *History of Cook County, Illinois.* Chicago: Goodspeed Historical Association–W.B. Conkey Company, 1909.

Illinois Bell Telephone Company. *Niles Center, Morton Grove, Lincolnwood Niles – Telephone Directory (1932–1946).* Chicago: The R.H. Donnelley Corporation, 1932–1946.

Krecioch, Michael. *Saint Hedwig and Me.* Lake City, FL: Allegro Press, 2001.

Niles Chamber of Commerce. *Directory (1959, 1962, 1969–70, 1971–72).* Niles: Niles Chamber of Commerce, 1959–1972.

Sweetow, Roberta Kaye. *Early Skokie.* Skokie, IL: Village of Skokie, 1976.

Tyse, Dorothy C. *History of Niles, Illinois.* Niles: self-published, 1973.

Zurawski, Joseph W. *Niles Centennial History: 1899–1999.* Marceline, MO: Walsworth Publishing Company, 1999.

Visit us at
arcadiapublishing.com

....